YO-EDP-596

THE GREAT AMERICANS SERIES

Thomas Jefferson

By Kathie Billingslea Smith

Illustrated by James Seward

Cover Portrait: Sam Patrick

Julian Messner
New York

Published by Julian Messner, a division of Silver Burdett Press, Inc., Simon & Schuster, Inc., Prentice Hall Bldg., Englewood Cliffs, NJ 07632.
JULIAN MESSNER and colophon are trademarks of Simon & Schuster, Inc. PRINTED IN MEXICO. 10   9   8   7   6   5   4   3   2   1

Library of Congress Cataloging-in-Publication Data

Smith, Kathie Billingslea.
    Thomas Jefferson / by Kathie Billingslea Smith ; illustrated by
James Seward.
        p.   cm. — (The Great Americans series)
    Summary: Examines the life of the multitalented man who is
remembered as the third president of the United States as well as
the writer of the Declaration of Independence and the founder of the
University of Virginia.
    ISBN 0-671-67512-5 (lib. bdg.) : $7.79
    1. Jefferson, Thomas, 1743-1826—Juvenile literature.
2. Presidents—United States—Biography—Juvenile literature.
[1. Jefferson, Thomas, 1743-1826. 2. Presidents.] I. Seward,
James E., ill. II. Title. III. Series.
E332.79.S64   1988
973.4'6'0924—dc19
[B]
[92]
                                      88-13629
                                      CIP
                                      AC

Thomas Jefferson was a remarkable man of many gifts and talents. Today, more than 150 years after his death, he is remembered as the author of the Declaration of Independence and the third President of the United States. But he was also a scientist, an inventor, an architect, a farmer, a diplomat, and the founder of the University of Virginia.

In 1962, President John F. Kennedy invited many Nobel Prize winners—top people in the fields of art, literature, and science—to a dinner at the White House. Before the meal, he spoke to his award-winning guests.

"You are the most extraordinary collection of talents...that has ever gathered together at the White House," he said, "with the possible exception of when Thomas Jefferson dined alone."

Thomas Jefferson was born on April 13, 1743 at Shadwell, his family's plantation on the banks of the Rivanna River in Virginia. He was the third of ten children born to Peter and Jane Randolph Jefferson.

Peter Jefferson was a sheriff and a member of the House of Burgesses. But he had the heart of a pioneer and spent several years surveying and mapping land in the Appalachian Mountains. He taught Thomas to love nature and to respect all people.

In 1745, the Jefferson family moved seventy miles east to help care for some relatives. It was here on a plantation called Tuckahoe that Thomas first began his schooling. At the age of five, he went with his older sisters to a nearby one-room schoolhouse.

Thomas was a tall, thin child with red hair and freckles. When he was nine, his parents moved back to Shadwell. Thomas went to live at a boarding school near Tuckahoe. He was an avid reader but also loved to be outdoors. Many days he could be seen studying and drawing different plants in the Virginia countryside. Thomas Jefferson seemed to notice everything around him.

In 1757, Peter Jefferson died. As the oldest son, fourteen-year-old Thomas inherited his father's large estate, his books, his surveying instruments, and a cherry desk and bookcase. According to his father's last wishes, Thomas promised to use his inheritance to get a good education.

Soon after that, Thomas moved to Reverend James Maury's log schoolhouse twelve miles away from Shadwell. There he studied Greek, Latin, English literature, geography, history, agriculture, and math. He was an excellent student. Thomas began collecting books and prized them above all his other possessions. He also learned how to play the violin and cello. Reverend Maury often took his students hiking and riding through the Blue Ridge Mountains in search of fossils. These were very happy years for Thomas.

In the spring of 1760, he enrolled at the College of William and Mary at Williamsburg. Williamsburg was the capital of the colony of Virginia. The country boy from the Blue Ridge Mountains was fascinated with the beautiful Governor's mansion there and the many shops lining Duke of Gloucester Street.

At age seventeen, Thomas was more than six feet tall and still growing. His friends called him "Long Tom." Long Tom had a gift for languages and learned to speak French as well as Greek and Latin. Later in life he also taught himself Italian and Spanish. He now had a fine collection of nearly 3,000 books.

Thomas graduated from college in 1762 and decided to become a lawyer. For five years he studied law books and worked with George Wythe, a well-known lawyer in Virginia, until he felt ready to practice law on his own.

At the age of twenty-four, Jefferson was admitted to the Bar of the General Court of Virginia. He handled many local cases and traveled on horseback all over Virginia.

▲ Monticello

Jefferson wanted a house of his own and made plans to build a home on top of a mountain near Shadwell. He called the spot "Monticello," which meant "little mountain" in Italian. In 1768, he leveled the top of the mountain and planted apple, peach, cherry, pear, fig and almond trees there. Then he drew up plans for a graceful red brick mansion with a domed roof and classical columns. The building and designing of this beautiful house were to be his pride and joy for years to come.

"Architecture is my delight," he often said, "and putting up, and pulling down, one of my favorite amusements."

The mansion at Monticello was not yet ready to live in when Thomas married a young widow named Martha Wayles Skelton on January 1, 1772. Thomas and Martha spent their first year together living in a one-room brick cottage next to the mansion. They called it "Honeymoon Lodge." Thomas imported an English piano for Martha for a wedding present. They often played duets together—she on the piano, and he on his violin.

In September of 1772, their first child was born. She was named Martha after her mother, but was nicknamed Patsy. A year and a half later, another daughter was born, but she died soon after birth.

◄ King George III

Courtesy of the Library of Congress, Washington, D.C.

Soon after his marriage, Jefferson gave up his law practice to spend more time supervising his four different plantations. He loved to experiment with growing different crops and claimed he was a farmer at heart.

Jefferson was also elected to serve in the Virginia House of Burgesses. Many colonists were unhappy that the King of England, George III, made them pay taxes to England, but did not let them have any say in governing themselves. In a paper called *A Summary View of the Rights of British America,* Jefferson wrote that the colonists had the right to set up their own government and write their own laws.

"The God who gave us life, gave us liberty at the same time...," he wrote.

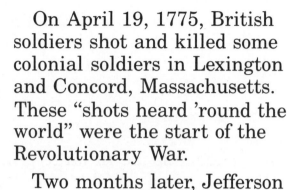

◄ John Adams

On April 19, 1775, British soldiers shot and killed some colonial soldiers in Lexington and Concord, Massachusetts. These "shots heard 'round the world" were the start of the Revolutionary War.

Two months later, Jefferson traveled to Philadelphia, Pennsylvania to attend a special meeting known as the Second Continental Congress. Philadelphia was the largest city in the colonies at this time. It had paved streets lit by whale-oil lamps, three libraries, a college and the only hospital in America. Representatives from all thirteen colonies gathered at the State House. At age 32, Jefferson was one of the youngest there.

◄ George Washington

The delegates quickly voted to organize an army and a navy to fight the British. George Washington was chosen to be the Commander-in-Chief of the colonial troops.

Jefferson formed a strong friendship with John Adams, a delegate from Massachusetts. The two men were quite different. Jefferson was tall and thin; Adams was short and plump. Jefferson seldom spoke in large groups. Adams was quite talkative. But this friendship was one that would last a lifetime.

In May, 1776, Jefferson was asked to write a formal statement declaring the colonies free and independent of England. At first he said that a more experienced statesman such as Adams should be the one to write it.

▲ Jefferson consulting (left to right) Roger Sherman, Benjamin Franklin, Robert Livingston and John Adams.

"No," Adams told him. "You write ten times better than I do."

Jefferson worked nonstop for more than two weeks. He wrote alone at a portable mahogany writing desk in a house on Market Street. John Adams and Benjamin Franklin stopped by to see him and offered a few suggestions. Jefferson wrote and rewrote the Declaration of Independence until he felt it was just right. The words he chose are ones that still ring true today.

"We hold these truths to be self-evident, that all men are created equal: that they are endowed by their Creator with certain unalienable

▲ Declaration of Independence

Courtesy of the Library of Congress, Washington, D.C.

rights: that among these, are life, liberty, and the pursuit of happiness."

In the Declaration of Independence, Jefferson stated that a government should protect the rights of its people and that when it did not "it is the right of the people to alter or to abolish it, and to institute a new government." He denied all allegiance to King George III and declared the "colonies to be free and independent states."

Late in the evening of July 4, 1776, the delegates voted to accept the Declaration of Independence. Word of the Declaration spread throughout the colonies. Bells rang in Philadelphia, and happy citizens pulled the British coat of arms down from the State House. In New York, patriots melted a statue of George III into bullets.

On August 2, the delegates gathered to sign the formal copy of the Declaration of Independence. One by one, they came forward and wrote their names on the document. If caught by British troops, the men knew they would be called traitors and put to death.

"Now we must all hang together," Ben Franklin said to the others, "or we shall all hang separately."

In September, Jefferson returned home to Monticello. Then, he went on to Williamsburg with his wife and little Patsy. For the next three years, Jefferson helped write 126 new laws for the state of Virginia. He was proudest of his Bill of Religious Freedom. It allowed Virginians the freedom to worship, or not worship, as they chose.

During these years, the Jeffersons lost two other babies, a girl and a

boy, shortly after
their births. But in August of 1778, a healthy daughter was
born. She was christened Mary and nicknamed Polly.

In June, 1779, the Virginia state legislature appointed Jefferson to be the Governor of Virginia. He moved to the new state
capital in Richmond. The Revolutionary War was still raging,
and Jefferson worked hard to send men and supplies to the colonial troops.

In January, 1781, British soldiers stormed through Richmond
and set fire to the city. Jefferson was forced to flee to Charlottesville, near Monticello. Even so, he was nearly captured by the
British cavalry and escaped only by riding through the nearby
woods that he knew so well.

▼ Surrender of Cornwallis.

In October, 1781, British General Cornwallis surrendered to General Washington at Yorktown, Virginia.

Jefferson's term of office as Governor of Virginia ended, and he returned to Monticello with his family.

"I have...retired to my farm, my family and books from which I think nothing will ever more separate me," he wrote to a friend.

Jefferson was happiest at Monticello. He had many interests. He enjoyed reconstructing skeletons from his collections of old animal bones. His gardens were another delight.

The mansion itself reflected the brilliance of its designer. Inside the house, Jefferson built hand-operated elevators to carry food from the underground kitchen to the upper floors. He constructed skylights in the bedrooms to let in more light.

Over the east entrance of the house, Jefferson built a large seven-day clock calendar with indoor and outdoor faces to tell the hours of the day and the days of the week. He was the first to design and build storm windows. He also invented a music stand that could be used by four musicians at once and a swivel chair and revolving writing table to make writing letters a more comfortable task.

In May, 1782, another daughter, Lucy Elizabeth, was born. She lived for three years. But Jefferson's wife, Martha, never recovered from Lucy's birth and became quite ill. She died four months later on September 6, 1782. Jefferson was grief-stricken and refused to leave his room for weeks. He never married again.

A year later Jefferson was chosen to be a delegate to the national Congress. The colonial money system at this time was a mess of different coins and bills. Jefferson introduced the decimal money system, based on units of ten, that we still use today.

In July, 1784, Jefferson and his friends, Adams and Franklin, were sent to Europe to work on trade agreements between the United States and France. When Franklin retired a year later, Jefferson became America's chief diplomat to France. He loved Paris—a city rich in culture and learning—but missed his home and friends in America.

"I...prefer the woods, the wilds, and the independence of Monticello to all the brilliant pleasures of this

▲ President George Washington

◄ President Thomas Jefferson

gay capital," he wrote to a friend from Paris.

In 1789, Jefferson and his two daughters, Patsy and Polly, returned home. George Washington had just been elected the first President of the United States. Jefferson served as his Secretary of State.

In 1796, John Adams was elected the second President of the United States. Jefferson became the Vice-President.

Four years later, in a close election, Jefferson was elected to be the third President of the United States. His inauguration was held in the new capital city of Washington, D.C. on March 4, 1801. Washington was a rustic village then. Pennsylvania Avenue, so impressive today, was an unpaved road that cut through patches of wilderness and swamp.

◄ Jefferson with French diplomats

As President, Jefferson served with great intelligence and common sense. He was determined to be a leader among his people rather than a ruler above them. He did not like titles such as "His Excellency" and asked to be called simply "Mr. President."

Unlike the President before him, Jefferson did not travel about town in a fancy coach, but instead rode on his horse, Wildair.

He gave no large state dinners—just small informal suppers. He loved ice cream, made from a recipe he found in France, and served it for dessert at almost every meal.

Jefferson enjoyed having his daughters and twelve grandchildren visit him in Washington. During one visit Patsy gave birth to the first baby ever born in the White House. The child was named after Jefferson's close friend and Secretary of State, James Madison.

While he was President, Jefferson's daughter Polly died. He was despondent.

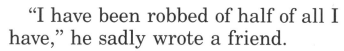

▼ Meriwether Lewis

"I have been robbed of half of all I have," he sadly wrote a friend.

In 1803, Jefferson doubled the size of the United States by purchasing the Louisiana Territory from France for 3 cents an acre. This additional land stretched America west to the Rocky Mountains.

Jefferson had always been interested in the American West and dreamed of a time when the United States might range from ocean to ocean. In 1804, he sent explorers Meriwether Lewis and William Clark to explore and chart the new Louisiana Purchase and lands west to the Pacific Ocean.

William Clark ▶

Courtesy of the Library of Congress, Washington, D.C.

That same year Jefferson was re-elected by a landslide to serve a second four-year term as President of the United States.

When his second term was over, Jefferson refused to run again.

"Never did a prisoner, released from his chains, feel such relief as I shall on shaking off the shackles of power," he said. Jefferson was pleased when James Madison was elected to be the next President.

After forty years of public service, Jefferson went home to Monticello to stay. He took charge of his farms again and began experiments with crop rotation. He redesigned many of his farm machines to work more efficiently. Jefferson and his old friend John Adams began writing to each other regularly.

Jefferson acted as an advisor to James Madison and James Monroe during their years as President. They were great friends of his and visited him as often as possible. In many ways they were like sons to him.

In his later years, Jefferson was able to realize one of his life-long dreams. He had always felt that a good education should be available to all people. In 1817, he purchased an old academy in nearby Charlottesville and founded the University of Virginia. Although he was in his late seventies, he designed the school's first buildings, planned the curriculum, hired talented teachers, and chose the books for its library. Each day he went down to the campus to oversee the construction. In 1825, the first students were admitted. Jefferson always considered the building of this university to be his finest achievement. When he grew too feeble to visit the campus each day, he had a telescope installed on a terrace at Monticello so that he could still see the school.

◄ James Monroe

Courtesy of the Library of Congress, Washington, D.C.

Jefferson became quite ill in the summer of 1826. On July 3, his condition worsened. He spoke his last words.

"Is it the Fourth?" he asked his doctor.

"It soon will be," the doctor replied.

Thomas Jefferson died at 12:50 on the afternoon of July 4, 1826—fifty years to the day after the acceptance of the Declaration of Independence.

His good friend John Adams died three hours later in Massachusetts, unaware that Jefferson had already passed on. "Thomas Jefferson still survives," were the last words he spoke.

Jefferson was buried beside his wife and children on the little mountain that he loved. According to his wishes, it simply says:

Here was buried
Thomas Jefferson
Author of the Declaration of American Independence
Of the Statute of Virginia for Religious Freedom
And Father of the University of Virginia